TAKE A CLOSER LOOK AT YOUR

Bones

BY ANN MALASPINA

The Child's World

Published by The Child's World®
1980 Lookout Drive • Mankato, MN 56003-1705
800-599-READ • www.childsworld.com

Acknowledgments
The Child's World®: Mary Berendes, Publishing Director
Red Line Editorial: Editorial direction and production
The Design Lab: Design
Content Consultant: Jeffrey W. Oseid, MD

Photographs ©: leonello calvetti/Shutterstock Images, 4;
Shutterstock Images, 5, 9, 11, 13, 16, 19, 20, 24; Alila
Sao Mai/Shutterstock Images, 7; Denis Radovanovic /
Shutterstock Images, 14; Andre Blais/Shutterstock Images,
15; iStockphoto, 17; sonya etchison/Shutterstock Images,
21; Photodisc, 23

Front cover: Shutterstock Images; Photodisc; leonello calvetti/
Shutterstock Images

ISBN: 978-1623235529
LCCN: 2013931355

Printed in the United States of America
Mankato, MN
July, 2013
PA02175

About the Author

Ann Malaspina is the author of more than 20 books for young people. She has written about jaguars, tsunamis, the Boston Tea Party, and many other topics. One of her first jobs after college was at a medical journal about bones and joints. She always wears a helmet when she rides her bicycle.

Table of Contents

CHAPTER 1

What Is Bone?

A skeleton hangs on the porch at Halloween. The chalky bones look stiff and dusty. They rattle and shake in the wind. Do our bones look like the skeleton's? Our bones do not rattle in the wind or gather dust. Bones are living organs, just like the heart and lungs.

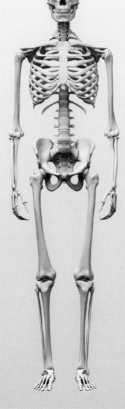

Unlike the skeletons we see around Halloween, our bones are alive.

Healthy living bones are strong and hard. They have important jobs to do. They give the body its shape. They also protect the organs inside our body. Bones are not solid like you might think. They are full of tiny holes for **blood vessels** and nerves. Bones have many layers.

Without bones, we would not be able to stand up straight or throw a ball.

Periosteum covers the outside of bones. It helps **muscles** attach to the bone. Underneath the periosteum is a hard layer of bone. Inside that layer is a spongy layer of bone that looks like honeycomb. In some bones, there is a thick jelly called **bone marrow**. Bone marrow stores fat and makes blood.

The smallest bone in the body is called the stirrup. It is inside the ear. It is smaller than an orange seed.

Bone

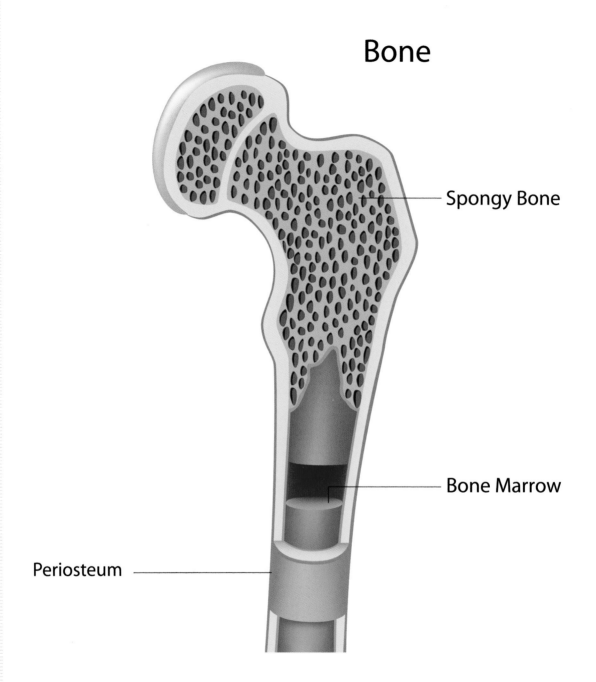

Spongy Bone

Bone Marrow

Periosteum

CHAPTER 2

What Do Bones Do?

Bones give us shape. Without our bones, we would fall to the ground. Just like a house protects us, bones keep the organs inside our bodies safe. The rib cage bones wrap around the heart and lungs like a shield. The hard skull protects the brain.

What is the only bone in your skull you can move? Hint: You use it to chew. Answer: your jawbone, or mandible.

Bones need other parts to do their job. **Joints** are the places where two or more bones meet. They hold the skeleton together and allow it to move. The ankle joint is where the leg and feet bones meet.

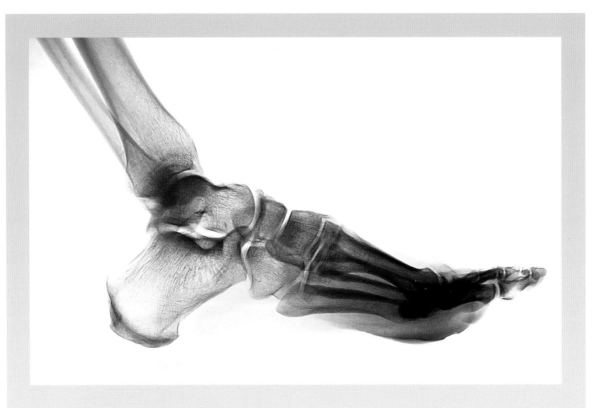

The ankle joint is like a hinge on a door. It lets you walk and run.

Ligaments connect bones to other bones. They are like strong strings. They stretch so bones can move. Bones need muscles to bring the body strength and power. Muscles are attached to bones with strong cords called **tendons**. Muscles help us fly a kite, dance, and even chew our food.

CHAPTER 3

Many Kinds of Bones

Bones come in different shapes. The thigh bone is called the femur. It is the longest, thickest, and strongest bone in the body. It helps us stand, run, kick, and swim. The ribs are thin and flat. They curve around the chest to protect the heart and lungs. The wrist has eight bones as small as marbles. They slide so you can twist your wrist.

Some parts, such as the foot, have many bones. The bones in your feet hold your weight when you walk. Three bones meet at the ankle joint. They rotate when we turn the corner or dance. Each big toe has two bones. The other four toes each have three bones. Toes keep us balanced so we do not tip over.

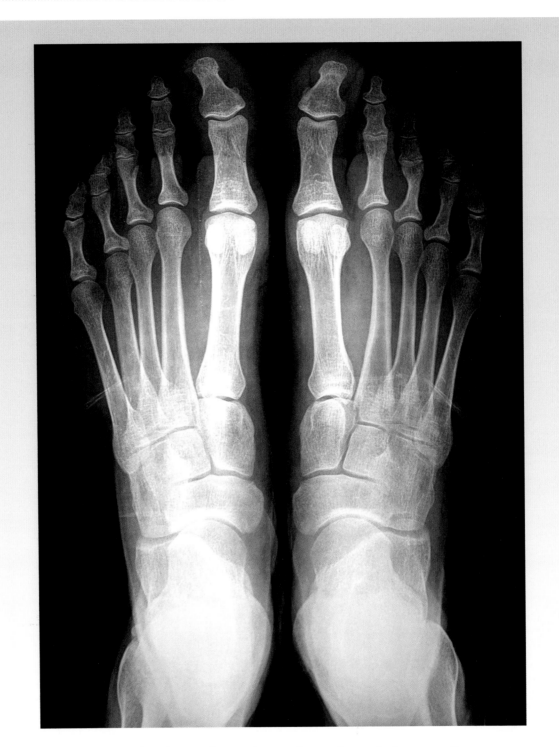

Each foot has 26 bones that work together to help you walk.

The skull is made up of two sets of bones. A thin but strong set of bones makes up the part that protects the brain. The other set makes up the frame of our face. It holds our ears, eyes, nose, and brain in place. It also protects them. The backbone, or spine, is made up of 26 small bones called **vertebrae**.

Babies are born with about 300 bones. Adults have only 206 bones. What happens to all those baby bones? They grow together as the baby grows.

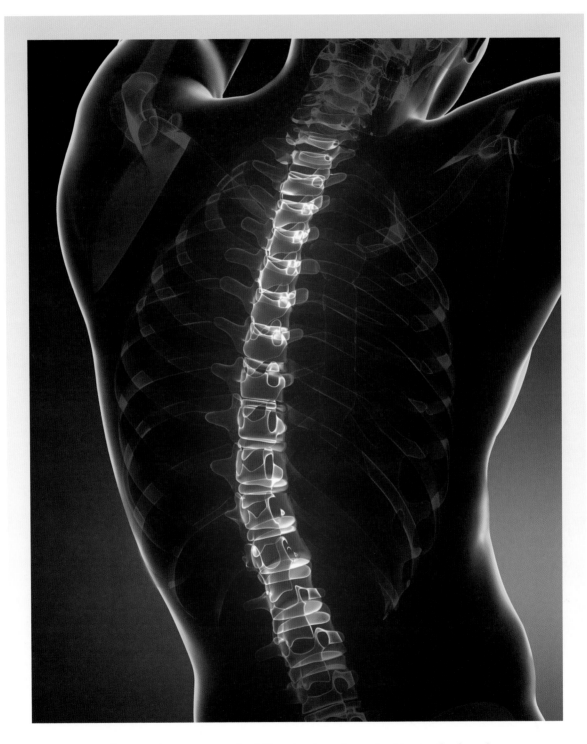

The vertebrae are stacked like checkers from the hips to the head.

The backbone protects the spinal cord, which sends messages to the brain. Joints between the vertebrae in the spine allow us to bend and twist.

Jellyfish are invertebrates.

Your spine is flexible, so you can curl into a ball for a somersault or bend backward.

CHAPTER 4

Sign My Cast

Have you ever broken a bone? Maybe you fell off your bicycle and landed on your wrist. Or maybe you twisted your ankle when you kicked a soccer ball. A bone can break if it is bumped, twisted, or put under too much pressure.

A broken bone can be scary. The area around the break might get swollen and tender. A doctor should see it right away. A doctor takes an X-ray to see if the bone is broken. A broken bone is called a **fracture**. The X-ray shows what kind of fracture it is.

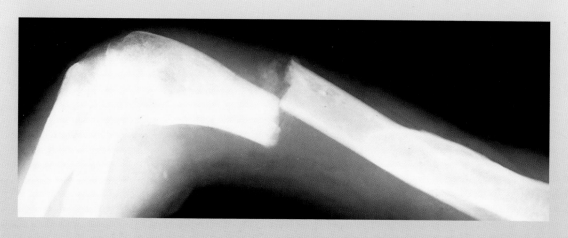

An X-ray shows where the fracture is on the bone.

The doctor makes sure the bone heals the right way. He or she might push the bone in place with his or her hands. Or the doctor might insert a pin to hold the broken pieces together. Oftentimes, a cast will be put on. A cast is a hard shell that protects the bone as it heals. Your friends will want to sign your cast. Broken bones can take weeks or even months to heal.

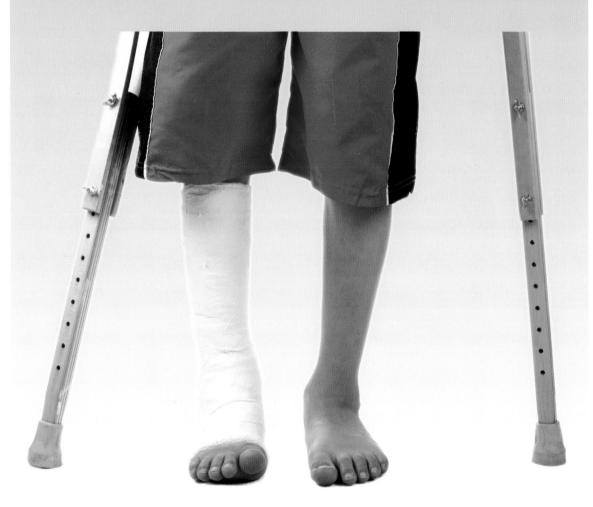

You might have a cast and use crutches for a broken ankle.

CHAPTER 5

Building Strong Bones

Bones keep growing until we become adults. If bones could talk, they would tell us to drink more milk. Milk has **calcium** and vitamin D, which your bones need to grow and stay strong. Without calcium, bones can become weak. Weak bones break more easily.

The best sources of calcium are low-fat milk and dairy products, such as cheese and yogurt. You can also get calcium by eating green vegetables, such as broccoli. Fish, chicken, and eggs are some other good bone foods.

People who don't get enough calcium can get **osteoporosis**. This is when your bones are not as strong and can break. Help keep the bones in your family strong by making sure everyone drinks milk with their meals.

Milk is a great, tasty source of the calcium your bones need to grow strong.

Bones need exercise every day to make them stronger. Get your bones moving. Take the stairs instead of the elevator. Walk to school instead of catching a ride. Join a sports team. Always wear a helmet when you ride a bike or skateboard. If you play football and other rough sports, wear gear and pads. Be careful when you walk on snow or ice.

Bones have to last a long time. People of all ages need to take good care of their bones. With plenty of exercise and a good diet, bones can stay strong and tough.

Wear the right gear to keep your bones safe and healthy!

Skateboarders must wear wrist guards, knee and elbow pads, and shoes.

blood vessels (bluhd VES-uhlz) Blood vessels are small tubes that carry blood. Bones are full of tiny holes for blood vessels.

bone marrow (bohn MAR-oh) Bone marrow is the thick spongy jelly inside bones. Bone marrow makes blood and stores fat.

calcium (KAL-see-uhm) Calcium is a mineral found in bones and teeth. Milk is a great source of calcium that helps bones grow strong.

fracture (FRAK-chur) A crack or break is called a fracture. Doctors call a broken bone a fracture.

invertebrates (in-VUR-tuh-brits) Animals without backbones are called invertebrates. An earthworm is an invertebrate.

joints (joynts) Joints are places in the skeleton where two or more bones meet. The ankle is a joint where three different bones meet.

ligaments (LIG-uh-muhnts) Ligaments are bands of tissue that connect bones and hold organs in place. The body needs ligaments to hold bones together.

muscles (MUHS-uhlz) Muscles are a kind of tissue in the body. Muscles are attached to bones so the body can move.

osteoporosis (AW-stee-o-pohr-oh-sis) Osteoporosis is when bones become weak and can break. Getting enough calcium can help keep bones strong so you do not develop osteoporosis.

periosteum (pair-ee-OS-tee-um) The outside layer of a bone is called the periosteum. The periosteum helps muscles attach to bones.

tendons (TEN-duhnz) Tendons are thick cords of tissue in the body. Tendons connect muscles to bones.

vertebrae (VUR-tuh-bray) The small bones that make up the backbone are all called vertebrae. Without our vertebrae, we would not be able to stand up.

BOOKS

Jenkins, Steve. *Bones: Skeletons and How They Work*. New York: Scholastic, 2010.

Macaulay, David. *The Way We Work*. New York: Houghton Mifflin, 2008.

Parker, Steve. *Skeleton*. New York: DK Publishing, 2004.

WEB SITES

Visit our Web site for links about bones: **childsworld.com/links**

Note to Parents, Teachers, and Librarians: We routinely verify our Web links to make sure they are safe and active sites. So encourage your readers to check them out!

INDEX

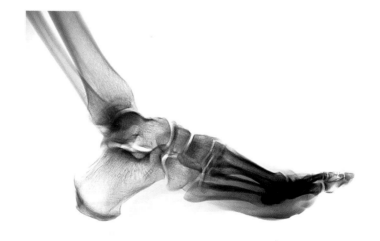

Take a closer look
at your bones /